Changing
Tempos™

Changing Tempos™

Erasing Victimization
Embracing True Love

Tiffany L. Samuel, Esq.

To order additional copies of this book, contact:
Xlibris Corporation
1-888-795-4274
www.Xlibris.com
Orders@Xlibris.com
65774

*Affectionately dedicated to
my parents, Toss and Mary Samuel III;
my siblings, Roderick, Cheryl and Mister,
along with their families;
grandma Lillie Mae;
and an infinite host of relatives, friends, students, and well wishers*

𝔚e've come this far by grace!

Amazing grace, how sweet the sound;
That saved a wretch like me;
I once was lost, but now I am found;
I was blind, but now I see.

—John Henry Newton

TWELVE DISCOVERY CHANNELS

(Directions: Read one a day and spread love!)

Preface..9
Preparing for this Journey..11

Stage One: IDIOSYNCRATION

Promises 14
Clichés 20
Don't Worry 28

Stage Two: INCAPACITATION

All This 36
Forced Abstinence 44
Run On 50

Stage Three: INTUITION

Hope Sparkles Again 56
An Autumn Night's Dream 62
Nuances 70

Stage Four: INTIMACY

Wisdom 78
Back To You 86
Soaring 92

Love Zone: "Reader Ponders" 99

Preface

Hello and thank you for your interest in this journey. Filled with gratitude, I am humbled by your desire to explore real challenges and solutions I continue to apply daily to live life more lovingly and abundantly. Blessed to share my story with you through the use of my original songs, I invite you to embrace music on a different level with me through this compelling written narrative.

From well over a decade of memories, I begin with the four stages of my personal development. Second, twelve discovery channels will reveal many experiences that inspired the songs shared throughout this journey. Third, each channel is divided into three realms necessary to adapt and overcome each experience, along with a season of change to identify the level of difficulty to cope with each channel. Last, each channel majestically marches into a love zone to essentially commit to heal and focus on a constructive plan for my future.

To grasp what you read, I ask simply that you open your hearts and minds to the mysteries of love and the divine power that can heal. Because love, in my opinion, is both a melody and a message, and this journal is a personal invitation to readers to fall head over heels, smile until your cheeks are red, laugh out loud, heal in silence, and wish upon a shooting star—in love with the open, hidden, blind, and unknown human being inside of yourself too. Peace!

PREPARING FOR THIS JOURNEY

Do you know someone who has been victimized? Could that someone be you? How do most people you know react to a personal crisis or tragic loss? Do they cry? Retaliate? Self-hate? Isolate? Wave that enormous white "victim's flag" and seek sympathy? Do they become the host of a lifelong pity party filled with regrets, bitterness, blame and anger at anyone who seems to be happy, successful, or positive about life?

Believe it or not, America is a wonderful place to live, with its countless freedoms; still, with vast opportunities for gain in this country, there are also great potentials for loss. For example, every day in America, a personal and property crime is committed against its citizens. As a result, Americans seem to ask the same haunting question: "How do we protect our homes, families, and personal effects from perpetrators (also known as perps) who could care less about our privacy, security, and peace of mind?" I too have been perplexed about what to do after an unfortunate encounter with crime and victimization.

Primarily, the goal of a "perp" is to gain. "Gain what?" you might ask. Well, the answer may alarm you. Maybe the perp wants your identity, child, money, car, laptop, sex, or maybe even your life. Ironically, some of these dangerous individuals in society may have been victimized in their past to some degree. Still, not every victim will become a societal perpetrator.

Ponder these questions: How many victims are there in the world? Can a victim also be identified as a survivor? What possible factors differentiate victims from survivors? The difference may well be the mindset of the person effected before, during, and after a crisis or tragedy. With startling statistics on the increase of personal and property crimes in our society, the susceptibility factor to victimization has become an indiscriminate multicultural, socioeconomic, and, in some cases, gender-neutral tsunami for all Americans.

Moreover, from years of research, observations, and self-study, I have developed three fundamental categories of victims. In part, from individuals who have been victimized and were willing to share their stories with me as well as my own insight derived from my life experiences, I have made a practical attempt to unravel the victim's complex. Throughout this journey, the complexities of victimization and these categories will be analyzed.

To begin, category 1 individuals never seem to recover, and though others may be harmed through an encounter with these individuals, the only lives they truly intend to endanger or destroy are their own. They disconnect from society, from their survival instincts, and choose to live with the mere basic needs of a human being. They never seem to adapt and persevere and don't believe they can receive love, understanding, or acceptance. Tragically, something just seems to be lost from their souls forever because they no longer fear and/or care about life or death. When you look into their eyes, they seem empty. When you touch them, they seem numb to human affection. When you talk to them, they respond with hostility or hypersensitivity, if they respond at all. In the end, they just want you to do whatever you came to do or say whatever you came to say so that they can engulf themselves back into their private little hells.

In comparison, category 2 individuals lack or deny themselves the adequate skills and services needed to essentially cope and resolve their thoughts and feelings about various painful experiences. As a result, they hurt themselves by default. Regardless of how much they desire to resolve their pain, category 2 individuals are consumed with fear and are their own worst enemies. This group consistently wastes time; second-guesses any- and everything, even if they know it to be true; makes excuses to avoid confronting their problems; and walks around in a cloud of confusion, unhappiness, and denial. Then, when their pinnacle degree of pain, disgust, and fatigue nearly destroys them, they enter into a possible danger zone and must choose life over death because only these two options remain.

In significant contrast, category 3 individuals, who are the survivors of the fittest, are self-motivated, highly resilient, and active. They seek justice, therapy, and counseling because they refuse to let victimization consume them. My story chronicles my journey through all three levels. Through my self-tailored movement entailing music therapy, knowledge gained from institutes of higher learning, and the key to unlocking my soul, divine intervention, I have been empowered to now share my journey from erasing victimization to embracing a true love.

STAGE ONE

Idiosyncration

I. DICTIONARY

Idiosyncrasy (noun)

Quirk
A way of behaving, thinking, or feeling that is peculiar to an individual or group, especially an odd or unusual one

Unusual response to something
An unusual or exaggerated reaction to a drug or food that is not caused by an allergy

Related words/terms
- ↑ Idiosyncratic (adjective)
- ↑ Idiosyncratically (adverb)

II. THESAURUS

Characteristic (adjective)

★Characteristic	★Personal	★Individual	★Distinctive
★All your own	★Eccentric	★Peculiar	★Particular

PROMISES

This song practically wrote itself.

Q: If I give you my heart, will you bring me
    grief?
A: Give me your heart, and, baby, I'll be so
    sweet.
Q: If I give you my time, will you reject
    me?
A: Give me your time, and I will gladly listen
    when you speak.
Q: If I care for you tenderly, will you misuse
    me?
A: Care for me tenderly, and I'll give you the
    best pampering.
Q: If I surround you with happiness, will I
    live in misery?
A: Surround me with happiness, and with you,
    I'll never be careless.

Music and lyrics © Tiffany Samuel   *Performed by Tiffany Samuel*

Discovery Channel: Promises
Season: Adversity

1

MENTAL REALM

Anyone who has ever wanted or needed anything from me for their own personal or professional gain, whether through benign or malicious intent, always promised me something.

"I'll pay you back your $354.62 when I get my check in two weeks!" "That was then, this is now—you've got to learn to trust me!" "I'll be right back with your car!" "If you marry me, I'll make you happy!" "I did not lie to you because I would never do that to a friend!" "I'll never hurt you, baby!"

A promise was my chance to love

and get what I wanted,

when I wanted,

and from whom I wanted it.

I could go on, but why? I really had to do some soul searching to discover why I entertained and allowed promises instead of results from people. No one needs to promise me a fact. I wrote this journal; this is a fact. My intention to write this journal two years ago was merely a promise to myself. However, my promise had no merit or factual basis until I produced some evidence or action. Therefore, I had to write this book to validate this promise to myself.

Indulging in wishful thinking and living in a false reality meant that I could create whatever ending I chose in my own little dream world. No one could control the outcome but me. I lived in the realm of a promise and dwelled on that promise no matter what the outcome was. For example, a promise to return home at a certain time meant that "real love" walked in the door at that promised time. Also, a promise to assist me with a project at work meant that "real trust" assisted me with the completion of that project at work. Even more so, a promise to wash my car, repay a loan, walk my dogs, rub my feet, or return my telephone calls were all promises of "real commitment" with the completion of those tasks.

So needy, I was willing to settle for less. So desperate, I was willing to live a lie. A voluntary victim, I was willing to cry. Just like a sad song often played on the radio, "I was looking for love in all the wrong places!" A promise was my chance to love and get what I wanted, when I wanted, and from whom I wanted it. No reality or outcome was going to interfere with my dysfunctional system of guaranteed love. I loved promises, and I received more than I could handle.

PHYSICAL REALM

Now, to take this self-assessment even further, I try to avoid cold climates for the entire year. Though my body temperature is within normal range, my body literally shakes with discomfort when exposed to environmental temperatures below seventy degrees. As a result, I am uncomfortable to the point of physical pain. Still I love nature. So it could not possibly do anything to hurt me, right? There had to be a medical reason as to why I must use a heater and electric blanket year-round, and I had to find the answer.

I wanted more answers,

more dialogue,

more understanding,

and yes, more love.

When I visited my primary care physician and took blood tests, she reviewed the results and told me that my blood levels were normal; and, that I was probably just cold-natured like her. Well people, that was just not good enough for me! I wanted more answers, more dialogue, more understanding, and yes, more love.

Therefore, I met with a hematologist, and he completed extensive tests on my blood cells. Guess what I found? You guessed it. NOTHING! Many years ago, I had self-diagnosed myself as an iron-deficient anemic because several women in my family were positive. Smart, right? WRONG!

Without a disorder, disease, condition, or illness detected in my 13 panel blood screen, I discovered that sometimes you cannot explain natural occurrences. I was just sent on my way and diagnosed "cold natured." Still I love nature, and I thought she loved me back, remember? Well, the specialist explained that the human body is an awesome creation and that medicine and science are not as precise. Thus, I immediately started researching the human elements in the body. I felt that nature was trying to tell me to take my self-love to another level.

I reviewed the periodic table of elements because I had forgotten them. In high school, I used to color the elements' chart in pretty shades of pastel. Anyway, I refreshed my memory on the twelve elemental groups and their respective percentages in the human body. Now, as I age gracefully, my goal is to monitor my elements to keep them within normal ranges to ensure my continued good health; otherwise, illnesses, diseases, disorders, and possibly death could result from my negligence.

For added measure, I incorporated this information into my music. Primarily, I paired up my songs with each elemental group based on how they relate to my mental, physical, and spiritual needs. Cool, right? Now I have a fun way to remember to balance everything in my life for daily optimal performance of my little five-foot physique.

SPIRITUAL REALM

I no longer attach my feelings to promises,

because they no longer represent a real commitment

and guarantee that someone will love me.

Consequently, this channel of adversity in my life was, of course, self-inflicted. Through this channel, however, I have come to understand and change many things about myself that I am grateful to have learned through experience as opposed to textual knowledge. Moreover, I am confident in my ability to solve my own problems, and I have emerged from this channel without bitterness. I am more responsible and wise.

Today, I can still entertain and accept promises with the proper documentation and collateral, or I can simply avoid the experience altogether. I no longer attach my feelings to promises because they no longer represent a real commitment and guarantee that someone will love me. I was searching for love, and I found a way to attach and expect every person, place, or thing promised to me to provide me with an opportunity to receive love. I know, crazy!

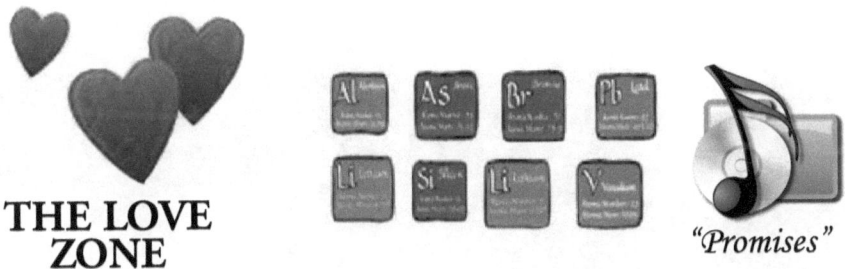

THE LOVE ZONE

"*Promises*"

My song "**Promises**" is paired up with the twelfth source in my body, which consists of the following eight trace elements: aluminum, arsenic, bromine, lead, lithium, silicon, strontium, and vanadium.

These elements are barely traceable in my body, and thus, they generally work together as one small collective group. Still they are important because they introduce my body to harmful elements in small doses. As a result, I will be able to identify and defend against them in the event of any exposure or misuse.

Accordingly, *promises* should be limited in the same way. The last thing I need to succeed is another promise. I understand this now; just like I understand that I also do not need exposure to arsenic, silicon, or lead. As for love, I still want love. It is still my passion and my purpose for living. However, I now know better than to base it on a promise.

CLICHÉS

This song was written during my period of rebellion and gullibility.

Some people will blatantly lie before telling the truth.
So let me add perspective to clichés I've heard since the days of my youth like:
-       *Don't start nothing that you can't finish.*
"Well, I'd rather walk away than get buried in it."
-       *And beauty's in the eye of the beholder.*
"Just behold someone else; this beauty doesn't need your help."
-       *The best things in life are free.*
"So why do people try to buy love, respect, and loyalty?"
-       *Easy comes and easy goes.*
"Well, I met that psychopath, and easy always came back for more!"

Music and lyrics © Tiffany Samuel   Performed by Tiffany Samuel

2

Discovery Channel: Clichés
Season: Resilience

MENTAL REALM

Why do people use clichés? We all have some rationale about why they are used; however, I believe that clichés are used by some people to manipulate others who cannot or will not trust and value their own belief systems or lack thereof. For example, I wanted everyone's love, so I valued, indiscriminately, what anyone who professed to love me believed regardless of their level of expertise.

The UNCF's motto

"A mind is a terrible thing to waste,"

should have been stamped

on my forehead throughout

most of my early adulthood.

In my opinion, clichés can be controversial for many reasons. First, the people who use these phrases are not the original authors. As a result, both the pseudo author and the ignorant listener must apply their own interpretations and perceptions to determine what is relevant to them. Second, clichés are not valid substitutions for evidence-based research. People who have quoted clichés to me to prove or disapprove a fact have categorically been challenged because a fact has merit without a cliché, whereas a cliché does not. Third, clichés can be used by some people as cunning and irresponsible attempts to influence insecure or naive people who desire wisdom and knowledge. The truth is that everyday experiences are challenging enough without the reckless abuse of these self-proclaimed experts with mouths full of clichés just waiting to unload on impressionable and vulnerable youth.

Still, I have witnessed people with their own decision-making and problem-solving challenges actually advise other people about the same problem they fail to resolve in their own lives. For example, clichés such as "No pain, no gain" and "Only the strong survive" have been uttered for years to encourage others to endure the challenges of everything from parenthood, college, financial debt, and health crisis. One conversation I recall with a young man entailed his correlation of his situation to the cliché "No pain, no gain." This young man shared his life's synopsis with me as follows: As a struggling single, he had dropped out of college twice and had decided not to reenroll a third time. Also, he had lost his last two jobs and was currently unemployed. Moreover, he had recently been notified by his ex-girlfriend that she was pregnant with his child.

Now, before I could respond to the magnitude of surmounting challenges he faced, this youngster just blurted out to me, "It's simple, Ms. Tiffany. No pain, no gain." He insisted that the cliché was a perfect phrase for his situation because he had suffered losses (i.e., his unemployment and college-dropout status), and yet he managed to still have a gain (i.e., his pending fatherhood). With great humility and disbelief, I just shook my head. I have encountered countless youths with this same unparalleled and misguided rationale.

Nonetheless, as a young woman, I too had difficulty understanding both clichés and my personal struggles. As a result, I allowed unnecessary influences to cause me pointless and avoidable hardships. Moreover, I was hurt and could only blame myself for using this dysfunctional process to receive love. The United Negro College Fund's (UNCF) motto "A mind is a terrible thing to waste" should have been stamped on my forehead throughout most of my early adulthood. I was far too concerned with leaving home for college and embracing my freedom and not concerned enough with developing my survival and coping skills to properly arm and prepare myself for the real world.

PHYSICAL REALM

This song was inspired by memories of both joy and pain. I was reared in a small town in central Louisiana where adults disciplined children and tried their best to encourage education. Still, the main control mechanism utilized by my parents and others in the adult community was biblical teachings, close adult supervision and discipline.

The 1970s, when I was born and reared, was also a challenging period due to corporal punishment, flawed school integration, and social and economic injustices, such that some adults used clichés as threats and warnings of pending dangers and unforeseen consequences. Adults seem to be specialists at using these phrases at just the right time to truly make their point painfully clear, such as "A hard head makes a soft behind" (i.e., buttocks) and "Don't let your mouth write a check that your behind can't cash" and "Don't start nothing, and there won't be nothing" and "You don't believe water is wet and fire burns" and "I'll beat the truth out of you [or the black off of you]" and "Since your head is hard as nails, your behind better be tough as leather" and "Give your soul to God because your behind belongs to me."

Ignorance or disobedience was more than bad;

it was evil.

Thus, it could only originate from one source

—the devil!

Nonetheless, I was reared in a diverse community, rich with multi-talented, blue-collar men and God-fearing, multitasking women. Most adults were courageous leaders, self-taught laborers, and strict enforcers of rules for safety and respect in our residential area. Still, my community was not perfect, which did have a psychological effect upon me as a child. For example, I witnessed some adults become frustrated and hopeless without support or options, while others seemed unable to cope after work-related injuries and/or family illnesses had seriously stifled their ability to maintain their livelihoods.

Also, as a child, I began to understand class divisions by observing my neighbors. Some neighbors, who had acquired more education, skills, and training and who had a large family support system, appeared to struggle less than others. These "lucky people," as I nicknamed them, seemed to enjoy moderate to significantly better lifestyles and opportunities. Meanwhile, the "rock climbing people," as I nicknamed those adults that seemed to be plagued with constant hardship, at times seemed to ventilate their pain through injurious words and actions toward their family, friends, and community. Still, no one ever seemed to hold a bitter grudge or seek intervention outside of our community.

So you may ask yourself this question: Where was Tiffany's family in this community that seemed to have examples of American growth and loss potential? Well, during our early years, we were "rock climbers," and though we were plagued with mayhem, we were sworn to secrecy and adamantly private. Eventually, with God's grace and mercy, we conquered most of our hard times and began to experience a little luck of our own. Through it all, we were a community of love that policed ourselves; while in simultaneous contrast, we were a community in pain that suffered in silence and denial.

On a note of nostalgia, I also learned many lessons during treasured visits to my grandparents' homes. One incident was at a corner convenience store near one of their homes whereby I was bewildered by yet another cliché: "How curiosity killed the cat." Perhaps overcome with temporary insanity, I had the audacity to ask a lady in that corner store why she slapped her daughter and made her cry when the little girl opened a pack of gum and put a piece in her mouth before her mother had paid the cashier. I was hurt for the little girl and told her mother that she was mean and unfair because I had seen her, the mother, grab a handful of grapes and eat them in the store without paying for them. Still, in my naïveté and dismay, I asked the lady why her little girl's action was worse than her own. I was trying to figure out if maybe grapes were of some superior food group or class and, thereby, was afforded some special privilege as opposed to the second-class gum.

Then, once the lady was outside the store, she told me that I had a "smart" mouth and began to yell at me as she said, "I am the adult, not you! You better stay out of grown folks' business. You talk too much, and the next time I catch you, I'm gonna beat your little mouthy behind." She turned to her daughter and said, "Do as I say and not as I do. Now get your behind in the car!" This stifling lesson was hurtful to her daughter and me because it clearly represented power over principle. In other words, dominance overrides discipline. Why? Because the parent (i.e., adult in charge) said so. Whether that little girl learned from her mother that ownership privileges, such as opening and chewing gum in the store, are not received until the item has been paid for is anyone's guess. Whether that mother paid for the grapes that she had consumed before leaving the store is another issue entirely.

SPIRITUAL REALM

Still, I had created a high emotional dependency on other people because I never trusted myself enough to value my own. In retrospect, I realize that all the pseudo wisdom and knowledge I relied on from others, like many of the clichés referenced in my song, really did not apply to my life. Most clichés neither proved nor disproved anything significant for me.

Nonetheless, I remained confused and devalued loving myself and chose instead to love everyone else for a major part of my life. Thus, to reach a level of resilience, I had to develop a personalized value system that would enable me to develop self-love, self-worth, and self-confidence. More precisely, I had to learn to trust and respect someone I barely knew—me!

Before this U-turn in my life, I was on a downward spiral. This spiral ended with my need to accept clichés as love offerings. After all, the people who so generously bestowed them upon me where the people I admired, cherished, respected, depended upon, and sometimes feared. I have traveled a long road searching for love, and it has redirected me back to reflect upon my past choices to now make better decisions for my future.

I realize that all of the pseudo wisdom and knowledge

I relied on from others,

like many of the clichés referenced in my song,

really did not apply to my life.

Clichés and **promises** were identical twins on an endless loop through their terrible twos for about half of my life. I bundled them up, gave them one central theme, taught them a sad song and dance, and then, proudly took them everywhere I went. They were dedicated to me, and I showered them lavishly with my time, energy, and loyalty. After all, we were one big family. Still, a change had to come.

One day, I actually began to think outside the box of this dysfunctional lifestyle. With so much love, I still could not understand why I was so depressed. What else was missing?

THE LOVE ZONE   *"Clichés"*

My song "**Clichés**" was paired up with the eleventh group of elements in my body, which consists of chlorine, cobalt, copper, fluorine, iodine, iron, manganese, molybdenum, selenium, and zinc.

These ten elements are found in my body at 0.70 percent. These elements support my immune system and maintain and regulate my fluid and cell balance in relatively low percentages.

Therefore, I limit my use of clichés in the same manner. Adults that have influenced me with **clichés** now have very limited power to persuade me. **Clichés** should not have been my primary solution to any circumstance I encountered. I had to learn to think for myself.

DON'T WORRY

This song was my mantra during a major turning point in my life.

When I'm giving my all and striving for success,
I use courage, commitment, and confidence.
My goal is not to win or lose, but it is to do my
*   very best.*
My journey to greatness takes more, not less of
*   my mind, my spirit, and my body, all put to*
*   the test!*
I don't condone envy or shame; I don't gossip or
*   blame.*
I'm too focused because I want a legacy behind
*   my name.*
Success is built by achieving my personal best—
not by destroying others with maliciousness.
I work and train to stimulate my brain to reveal
*   the message, "No pain, no gain!"*

Music and lyrics © Tiffany Samuel   *Performed by Tiffany Samuel*

Discovery Channel: Don't Worry
Season: Metamorphosis

3

MENTAL REALM

I love to create, organize, and implement projects. However, when the explosive mix of physical, mental, and emotional challenges culminated into one overwhelming, adamant obstacle, I again had to renew my spirit and strengthen my character for yet another emergence of unwelcomed adversity. During this time, I was pursuing my law degree. With research skills, projections goals, a business plan, client leads, and a potential list of investors, I was geared for an exciting career upon graduation and bar passage. However, when I was hit by a driver allegedly under the influence during this critical time in my legal studies, I had no courage or will to survive this major crisis. I wanted out of the game. I just wanted the suffering to move on to the next person. I had had enough of pain.

I learned an important lesson about people:

Even with the best intentions, people will only help

and be dependable for a short period of time

before they return to their own lives and agendas.

Unexpectedly, my colleagues and associates began offering criticism as opposed to encouragement during my recovery. I was unprepared and shocked by their opposition and lack of solidarity. More so, I was further saddened by the realization that some people were relieved that I was too injured to compete for career advancement opportunities in the workplace. The corporate world is a circus because it is full of clowns, ringmasters, jugglers, and beasts.

Further disappointment came when some of the closest and most important people to me sometimes hesitated or did not even stop their lives to help me. People were supposed to love me, right? After all, everyone was always so eager to tell me how much they loved and appreciated me. So what was the problem? Why did I feel so abandoned? Why did I feel so rejected?

The reality was that other people had faced challenges and setbacks just like I did. When someone said that they loved me, I chose to view their verbal declaration as a bona fide, enforceable service agreement. Erroneously, I believed that their love meant that they would be available to assist me if I ever needed them. I learned an important lesson about people: Even with the best intentions, people will only help and be dependable for a short period of time before they return to their own lives and agendas.

PHYSICAL REALM

I could tell you that I handled my personal and professional challenges with dignity and grace, but it would not be the truth. After years of procrastinating and avoiding my problems, I just caved in under the pressure. I felt like my life had ended when all my plans seemingly failed.

Though struggling to cope with constant pain and discomfort, permanent injuries, depression, and a twenty-pound weight gain were difficult enough; I still tried not to let the hardships totally destroy my spirit. This period of suffering is at times inexplicable. After three years of an unspeakable and pathetic existence, I finally asked God for the strength to stop whining and wishing I was dead.

As I prepared myself for my day in court, I reflected over the long, grueling three years it took to finally bring my case to trial. With allegations of fraud, witness tampering, insurance company stalling tactics, failure to appear for deposition notices against the defendant, medical bills over six figures, multiple medical procedures, and countless hours of legal research and document preparation, I was exhausted. Uncertain about my reactions to seeing the defendant again, I was guarded against any last minute schemes and maneuvers that had been standard practice for him.

Upon entering the courtroom, I looked around at the team of lawyers, witnesses, and parties seeking recovery. Then, I noticed an unfamiliar woman standing near the defendant's table wearing a neck brace. Unbeknownst to me, this woman was the defendant's wife who the defendant had attempted to murder on the previous night. When I looked again at her, she looked at me with an expression that made me feel like perhaps I had been spared the worst pain that the defendant could inflict. I felt connected to her because of a tragic commonality—pain and victimization.

Thereafter, the defendant was escorted into the courtroom from jail detention in his orange jumpsuit with his hands and feet shackled in chains. I was dumbfounded, and I felt like I was in a twilight zone! The defendant had been charged with attempted murder and was being held without bail pending his adjudication.

During my trial, I remember sitting in the witness box and telling the judge that I was a "shell of a woman" . . . lost in my pain. When I looked over at the defendant, he stared at me without remorse or empathy and in a nonchalant manner. At times, the defendant laughed, smirked and even told the judge during his testimony that no one understood all he had been through. I was disgusted and defeated by the whole experience.

Further humiliation and shame was revealed during the trial as I had to describe my permanent breast scars and knee conditions that affected the clothes I could wear and the activities I could no longer enjoy. I explained how the pain was constant and aggravated by seemingly everything from the weather to basic daily activities. For example, after several surgeries, my knees still perpetually malfunction, because there is no corrective treatment or procedure to remedy my condition. Now, I have modified my lifestyle by regulating every lengthy period of sitting and standing to avoid increased pain.

After the trial, I looked over to the defendant's wife again, but by this time, I thought to myself, "We are all victims. I don't want to be a member of this group anymore. The victims' box is too crowded." At that moment, I felt claustrophobic and finally felt motivated enough to escape from victimization and shift into a new liberating mode—survivor of the fittest.

In a battle to survive,

the time had come

to give myself a second chance.

I wrote this song "Don't Worry" and switched from physical therapy to swimming for strength training. Also, I embraced a diverse group of medical and fitness professionals for guidance and put everything else on hold. In a battle to survive, the time had come to give myself a second chance.

SPIRITUAL REALM

Surprised and unprepared for the realization that people just went on with their lives as if I did not even exist, I was flabbergasted and hurt because I wanted their love. I wanted everyone to love me so much that I begin to care for myself by default. I cared and loved myself only after accepting the fact that no one else around me wanted the job. This is a sad but true fact.

After years of soul searching

and what seemed like endless waiting,

God gave me the strength to forge ahead

to a new beginning.

After every other viable option failed, I shamefully chose God as a last resort. To move toward reconstructing my life, I prayed for divine intervention to resist the urge to continue my pattern of self-destructive thoughts and behaviors. To focus my mind on embracing optimism, I really begged God to help me. After years of soul-searching and what seemed like endless waiting, God gave me the strength to forge ahead to a new beginning.

During and after my lowest hours of depression, anger, failure, disability, broken-heartedness, and victimization, I had to learn to forgive myself for giving up on my life. I finally cared that I was alive, and it felt good. Now, I wanted everything back and more. With the development of a more personalized system to cultivate courage, energy, healthiness, and love, God gave me the strength to persevere.

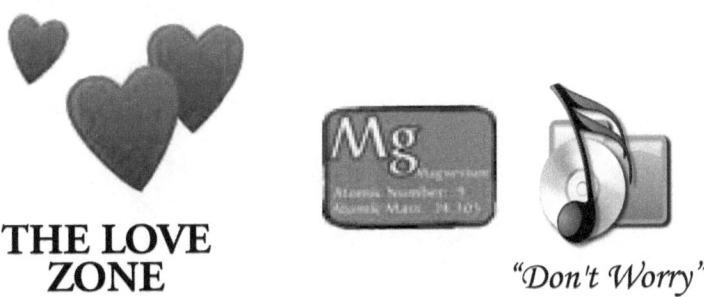

THE LOVE ZONE   *"Don't Worry"*

My song "Don't Worry" was paired up with the tenth elemental source in my body, magnesium. My body supplies 0.05 percent of magnesium because only a small amount is required for proper growth and the formation of my bones, muscle tissues, and enzymes. This element helps my nervous system to function.

As a result, I strive to live drama and stress free and to keep a can-do attitude to help contribute to my overall good health. Likewise, my commitment to God was to incorporate positive self-talk and disassociate myself from negative people. Now, I have mental fortitude instead of nervous breakdowns.

STAGE TWO

Incapacitation

I. DICTIONARY

Incapacitate (transitive verb)

Deprive of effectiveness
To deprive somebody or something of power, force, or effectiveness;

Officially rule somebody out
To disqualify somebody or make somebody legally ineligible

Related words/terms
♠ Incapacitation (noun)

II. THESAURUS

Debilitate (verb)

★ Debilitate   ★ Injure   ★ Harm   ★ Put out of action
★ Lay up   ★ Enable (Antonym)

ALL THIS

This song illustrated my personal struggle to endure the challenges of an unhealthy relationship.

*I feel special at times then like a plain Jane;
when we're normal and content, everything
turns strange
with moments of craziness, and I know I'm sane.
Hopefully, we'll grow, even though I'm
drained.
I feel pleasure beneath unspoken pain of broken
hearts from mistakes we've both claimed.
Still, I'm burdened by thoughts that we'll never
change.
And I'm torn and sentimental that we remain
and all this is because I . . . I love you!*

Music and lyrics © Tiffany Samuel *Performed by Tiffany Samuel*

4

Discovery Channel: All This Season: Adversity

MENTAL REALM

Just when I thought that the worst was over for me emotionally and that I could relax my defenses, a special delivery of "killjoy" (i.e. relationship warfare) arrived at my door! Like many people who desire love, I had to learn to take the good times along with the bad ones. Nonetheless, I still struggled sporadically with volumes of painful memories that always seemed to rekindle my fears about trust and commitment.

To begin, without a healthy dose of self-worth

as an essential defense mechanism,

I could not exercise the rationale

needed in my past to sever

unhealthy relationships.

In addition, my adult dysfunction was further perpetrated by past childhood isolation and confusion whereby more emphasis was always placed on my mistakes and failures at home in such a traumatic rampage of anger, violence, and banishment that I felt unworthy of living and experienced severe depression. Gratefully, God was merciful and long-suffering with me along with the prayers for and over my life by friends and family. Now, I have begun the internal cleansing necessary to resurrect my belief in relationships, and my pilgrimage to self-efficacy has enabled me to laugh at myself and rejoice for what remains of my life as opposed to crying and mourning over my losses.

To begin, without a healthy dose of self-worth as an essential defense mechanism, I could not exercise the rationale needed in my past to sever unhealthy relationships. Largely in part because I learned one counterproductive principle as a child: to expect violence and belittlement anytime I disappointed or failed to meet the expectations and/or demands of my parents, my father in particular. Normally, my father achieved this point of satisfaction and peace with me usually after he had consumed a few drinks, beaten me for at least an hour, and then canvassed over his work product, while my mother bandaged me properly. My father told me that he acquired his violent behavior from his parents, and my father's mother, in turn, told me that she also had to endure maltreatment from her father. Tragically, I knew I had been drawn into a cycle of violence, and I desperately wanted to escape.

From my horror files, I still remember one of my father's discipline tools: a two-by-four piece of wood, wrapped in gray duct tape, with the written phrases "Thanks, Dad" on one side and "More, Dad" on the other. The gray tape was added as a note of genius because the boards usually broke easily without this structural enforcement. Nonetheless, the proper execution of this correction tool was to perform a home run swing, like with a baseball bat, using both hands until the tool connected to the targeted area—my buttocks and/or thighs to be exact—where it remained for a few seconds for maximum overall pain and discomfort. There were a few instances when I managed to receive almost twenty contact swings before I tried to escape or beg to die. Please allow me to abruptly end this portion without proper transition.

As an adult, I became focused on pleasing others until they were happy, pleasant-natured, proud, and satisfied with my thoughts and actions. Needless to say perhaps, I became a socially dysfunctional adult in relationships as well. Once, I fell into a month long bout of hopelessness and depression because I could not convince my partner to leave me, although subconsciously I knew that I should have severed the relationship as opposed to enduring his abuse and betrayal. Moreover, I lived with and through the experience with private depression, humiliation, and shame because I had lost even the faith I had in God as a child to protect and rescue me from a miserable adolescence. As an adult, I gave up on Godly intervention and just kept praying to die in my sleep, to take me out of my misery.

Now with full accountability for what happened to me,

I understand that I gave implied authority

to harm me by remaining in an abusive relationship.

Now with great understanding about abuse, neglect, and psychological warfare, I can heal from the painful afflictions I allowed in that relationship: name-calling, infidelity, perpetual absence, perversion, and pessimism (i.e. dissatisfaction with any- and everything I said, did, cooked, wore, and thought.) Still, I have to ask myself, one more time, "Why did I stay, and how could I have been so blind?" The only answer I could give myself then was that my adult relationship did not involve violence, so I felt a sense of accomplishment and freedom from my childhood experiences and fears. The answer I give myself now is that I lacked the knowledge and understanding to protect myself then; however, today with God's protection and mercy, I am empowered to demand better treatment from others as well as from myself.

Unaware of the damage I had caused myself by accepting the systemic abuse, I have since learned how to cope with the pain I allowed into my life. Now with full accountability for what happened to me, I understand that I gave implied authority to harm me by remaining in an abusive relationship. Moreover, this relationship, in particular, was inherently co-dysfunctional because my partner sadistically chose to stay in our relationship to abuse me rather than love or leave me, and I chose to endure anything except violence rather than demand better treatment or leave him. Now on hindsight, I recognize how I set myself up as an easy target. Analogously, I was a bull's-eye at close range, and his semiautomatic "rifle of lovelessness" blew a hole right through me! How's that for visual imagery?

In retrospect, I was completely unaware that I set my treatment guidelines too low for a man to respect and cherish me. With great clarity, I have learned that healthy people in relationships do not live with and love one another with a constant fear of abuse and neglect. In fact, healthy people in relationships can sometimes have disagreements and challenges that either strengthen their commitment or inevitably sever their union. Still in all, no one expects or settles for abuse or neglect as a normal condition or occurrence in a healthy relationship.

On another note of reflection, it is clear to me now that nothing would have ever been good enough for this man I truly loved. Left with a complete feeling of worthlessness, this man finally told me after many years that he never loved me. When I finally left him, I was numb, dumb, and overcome with bitterness. Determined to hide the annihilation of my being, I cocooned myself into an invisible force field, labeled "emergency pain relief escape pod." I began to mourn and grieve for the hurt woman inside of me. Then, I had to deal with my rage and learn to forgive us both.

A situation of this destructive magnitude clearly had two willing participants. It no longer mattered who was more at fault because it was time to heal. When he called to apologize one day, I told him that my love was unconditional and that I had forgiven us both. In the end, my love was pure because I had found peace and release from the negative feelings I felt for him. Now on a survivor's path and out of my victim's box, I breathed a sigh of relief.

PHYSICAL REALM

Having paid in full, bought lessons shelved in my heartbreak file cabinet, I was well guarded against men who exemplified qualities, expressed or implied, that seemed detrimental to my health and happiness. Still, even though I was too reluctant to give men the benefit of the doubt, I still made a conscious effort to be considerate of their feelings and chose my words of rejection very carefully as male suitors came whistling their "I'm a good guy" tune. Nonetheless, several men entertained me with their style, charisma, intellect, and wit; however, none of them seemed to warrant my love and trust.

Paranoid and horrified of another broken-heart,

I began to play relationship dodge ball.

Ironically, I still wanted a man to genuinely love me, in theory, although I did not believe, in actuality, that there was a man on the planet that qualified. Paranoid and horrified of another broken heart, I began to play relationship dodge ball. In other words, I scrupulously dealt with men as a wise person might handle potentially hazardous material. Most times, I simply ran in the opposite direction until I wore myself out. My strategy was to engage and disengage with others before they could hurt me first. I was on the offense and defense simultaneously, which meant that I always made the first and last move. Even with a great need to end this grueling cycle of fear, I was not willing to take any risks.

A wholehearted lover of everyone else, I still neglected myself at times and was too lost to evoke enough common sense to love and heal my internal wounds. Though my friends and family tried to save me, I chose to lose. Though my career tried to lead me toward a constructive path, I chose not to follow. To win, I had to leave my stubbornness behind and stop wallowing in defeat.

SPIRITUAL REALM

Now in the passenger seat of my wrecked vessel,

I began the long and grueling journey to listen,

learn, love, and live with divine purpose.

Though God has always loved me unconditionally, my misguided loyalty was synonymous with the biblical account of sinners who chose Barabbas over the son of God, Jesus. Needless to say, I did not feel like I deserved forgiveness, and even worse, I did not know how to even ask God for redemption after I betrayed him. At a time like this, my only option was to redirect my actions and energies toward something pleasing to the only man who could spiritually save me from myself—God. Now in the passenger seat of my wrecked vessel, I began the long and grueling journey to listen, learn, love, and live with divine purpose.

As time passed, I began to commit to addressing my issues of rejection and fear. I also learned to appreciate and accept new philosophies and practices that were easier to maintain and less stressful on my heart. With more control over my emotions, I stopped overdramatizing life. Likewise, trials, tests, and tribulations no longer felt like curses over my life. To keep my life in alignment with God, I worked hard to set daily goals and standards for healthier living.

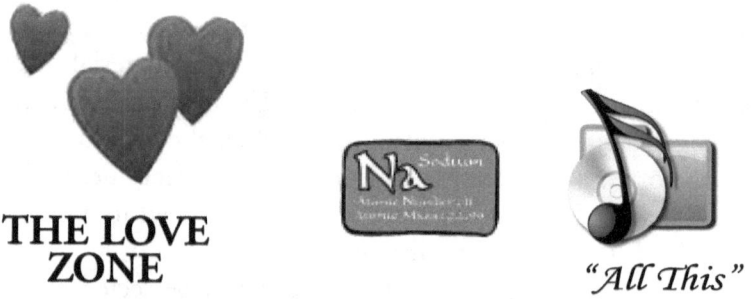

THE LOVE ZONE

"All This"

My song **"All This"** was paired up with the ninth elemental source in my body, sodium. Again, the percentage is relatively low at 0.15; however, sodium is needed for fluid balance. Accordingly, I now control my sodium intake, and thus consume it only in small doses.

I understand that my adversity, like sodium, was needed for my growth; however, an overdose could have been fatal. To develop a stronger sense of character, I work daily to improve. In retrospect, my song **"All This"** and sodium are definitely two of a kind. They both have taught me to set boundaries and require and live within those limits.

FORCED ABSTINENCE

This song was written during a phase where I chose to love on the side of caution.

I want to share emotions with you. I want to fulfill profound needs with you.

I want to understand, if I can, how to take your precious hand.
And learn to trust someone new; though, it's hard for me to do.
Would you sacrifice for more than your trade or degree?
Do you desire more than a woman with a great face or body?
Are you God-fearing with a positive personality?
Do you desire more than to be rich and cool?
Could you be another player on the loose?
Are you whole inside with a strong desire to live right?

Music and lyrics © Tiffany Samuel   *Performed by Tiffany Samuel*

Discovery Channel: Forced Abstinence
Season: Resilience

MENTAL REALM

To my dismay, I emerged onto the adult dating scene and encountered more men who were desperate to marry and start a family or who were sexually motivated for selfish gain than those who sought out gradual friendships with the potential to become committed partners. As a result, I found myself in perpetual hibernation from dating, relationships, and sex. While on this subject, my exposition on sex is simple:

Sex is commitment and responsibility—

all rolled into one big dose of reality.

As a result, I just could not and will not settle for sex as "the great alternative" to what I truly desire: a lifelong relationship with a God-fearing man who possesses wisdom, honor, faithfulness, and accountability for his actions as a matter of his personal constitution. Unfortunately, instead of men recognizing my yearning for an authentic connection, I have been either pursued or ridiculed as a challenge, a tease, a trophy, or a prize.

Though I have read countless books and engaged in various discussions about intimacy, I still have not uncovered the mystery behind the breakdown in various forms of communication between men and women in relationships. Perhaps relationship therapists, counselors, and psychologists also seek answers to the ongoing ambiguity.

Again, in my opinion, sex is not the "Great American Pastime"; therefore, I refuse to treat it merely like a leisure sport. Consequently, I choose to abstain from a mere sexual relationship. I feel this way for many reasons. One reason is that my parents really drilled into my head, through countless lectures and their continuous example of love and fidelity, that sex is not practice or a test to determine readiness for real-life commitments and responsibilities. Sex is commitment and responsibility—all rolled into one big dose of reality.

Another reason is because sex did not mask or fill the serious voids and inadequacies in my adult relationships: financial debt, lack of communication and attentiveness, and lack of support and acceptance. Without a constructive plan to effectively remedy these relationship barriers, sex could not seal or buffer the lack of cohesion in my relationship. In my opinion, sex may perhaps function as the relationship glue for some people; however, sex is absolutely not the relationship engine!

An adamant point of disagreement or a complete deal breaker for me is a man who insists that he must have sex as a prerequisite for "real love" and as an essential component to the sustainment of that love. To my disappointment, men who can bond without testing my reflexes of disgust and rejection have been a rarity on my journey to find love. For example, one man who pursued me actually told me that most women usually pursued him because he was a wealthy doctor. Cynically, he joked that he liked to tap women on their heads to see if their legs would spring open like a gate to get his wealth. He could never hold a decent conversation without a joke about sex, his career, or his finances, yet he claimed to not understand why I never returned his phone calls.

Though there are many men who may understand that women are not conquests, I have only experienced this with my male friends, not men who pursued me as a love interest. Thus, to avoid another disappointment, I became a private investigator, surveillance expert, and psychological profiler. My goal was simple: to dissect and disconnect from the source that had caused me so much pain—the alpha male.

PHYSICAL REALM

On a different note, I have pondered for many years to finally understand why sensuality is more important to me than sexuality. For some men and women, I understand that sexuality is the important component or principle of pleasure. In fact, some people have shared with me that sensuality and sexuality are inclusive, while others believe they are notably different. I am of the latter view for many reasons.

I have pondered for many years to finally understand

why sensuality is more important to me than sexuality.

To begin, sensuality to enhance a bond with someone I love, by my own definition, is metaphysically different from sexuality. When my past relationships lacked affection and effective communication, sex intensified my sadness, discomfort, and loneliness. Simply put, I was disconnected and unfilled. With more time anticipating the empty feeling inside that usually surfaced before, during, and after sex in my relationships rather than enjoying whatever pleasure I could from the physical act, I just wanted to say, "Stop . . . Not this again," and crawl inside myself and disappear.

To the contrary, I can genuinely enjoy sensuality because this pleasure is derived from both self-pleasure as well as partner intimacy for me. For example, I enjoy self-pleasure while curled up at a bookstore with a great book; during warm, soothing bubble baths or swimming; while burning aromatherapy candles; whenever nourishing my skin and injuries with lotions, oils, and therapeutic massagers; or while listening to relaxing music. Likewise, I enjoy partner intimacy when my partner holds my hand, reads to me, and falls asleep in my arms while cuddling during a movie. For these precise reasons, sensuality is a top priority and truly satisfying and, at this point in my life, does not require sex to predicate or validate.

SPIRITUAL REALM

I love men and will continue to believe and pray

that every man can embrace

the whole human journey of purposefulness

and love with a like-minded woman

to fulfill whatever is to become their unified destiny.

So am I any closer to a light bulb moment in my journey to find a love that's right for me? The answer is no. Do I understand now what lies between the galaxy of men and women or can I explain the widely used analogies of "women are from Venus, and men are from Mars?" The answer is no. Therefore, the ***relationship equation*** for me is simple: If I still do not know or understand ***men*** and the way they love, which represents x, and I still have so much more to learn about ***myself*** and how I need to be loved, which represents y; then, ***sex***—the great on-your-back experience—which represents ***the unknown variable***, neither correctly or effectively solves this equation. This is my opinion, and I am not seeking any input, in support or opposition.

So in the end, I would not go as far as to say that I am confident that I know and understand men. However, I will say this: I love men and will continue to believe and pray that every man can embrace the whole human journey of purposefulness and love with a like-minded woman to fulfill whatever is to become their unified destiny. Moreover, love is a powerful, natural force that elevates men and women above their earthly differences to a spiritual state of humility and sacrifice despite their human flaws and insecurities. To this end, I believe that every human wants someone to share a bond with together on this planet.

THE LOVE ZONE

"Forced Abstinence"

My song "**Forced Abstinence**" was paired up with the eighth elemental source in my body, sulfur. This element is produced in my body by amino acids and B vitamins at 0.25 percent. Sulfur aids in my bone growth, blood clotting, and muscle metabolism. Likewise, it counteracts toxic substances in my body.

I believe that sulfur is the perfect partner for my song "**Forced Abstinence**" because I consider it to be very potent, just like sex. As a great enhancing ingredient in a healthy, monogamous relationship, sex should still not substitute for unconditional love and support. As a result, I want to be loved for life, instead of sexed to death. There will be no compromise. Sex will just have to wait for my soul's sake.

RUN ON

*This song was written based upon my daily prayer
to renew my courage and faith.*

*I've had the chance to see some of the best and
  worst of times literally.
When plans went bad or love turned sad, the
  only hope that I had was God created me
  built to last.
So holding on, one day would make me glad to
  open my eyes to see a brand new day
to start all over loving and living in a healthy
  way.
I'll run on to see what the end will be.
I'll run on to see what's in store for me.
I'll have courage to run on to fulfill my
  destiny.
I'll have faith to run on to my new beginning.*

Music and lyrics © Tiffany Samuel   *Performed by Tiffany Samuel*

Discovery Channel: Run On
Season: Metamorphosis

MENTAL REALM

In the dream world that I lived in most of the time, I set world records, was historically significant, dazzled the world with my multiplicity, made more money than I could possibly spend, and saved the world with my benevolence and humanity. With great sadness, I could not possibly live up to the expectations in my dream world; thus, I felt most days like a failure.

What changed? I stopped dreaming of achieving greatness and began proactively working to make small changes to my situation one day at a time. I stopped waiting on a great event or great recognition to jump-start my career and just decided to make everyday miracles happen in my life one project at a time. I stopped loving everybody else's beauty, wealth, family life, career, physique, and talents and decided to seek my own success in these areas.

I stopped dreaming of achieving greatness

and began proactively working

to make small changes to my situation one day at a time.

Less worried about my record of wrongs, I now triumph over my countless opportunities to do so much better with my life. Tears of pain are replaced with laughter for all I hope for tomorrow. More than my mistakes and failures, I take leaps of faith to achieve even the slightest of goals for myself. I love who I am and the direction I now travel—forward.

PHYSICAL REALM

One evening, as I sat down to play my piano for my number 1 fans, my two dogs, I began to cry as feelings overwhelmed me while singing about my pain and playing chord progressions. Then, a friend came by to visit, and she also began to reveal her personal and professional woes. Then, instinctively, I played this song for her. We cried, hugged, and laughed, and she told that this was her song too. To this date, I still dedicate this song to her.

Still, I feel so much better about myself just knowing that I only have to please God, not to receive his love or forgiveness, but to honor him. No person has the profound capability to love and accept me unconditionally to the degree of God's fervent devotion. For this compelling reason, I now understand why another person should never have dominion over my life.

Empowered now to run on, something inside of me will not stay down. A gentle whisper in my ear will not settle for less. A virtual dream keeps playing in my head that looks too easy to claim and to receive, and now I believe. God has activated my internal green light, and now I talk, smell, taste, feel, and see from within my soul. It seems some days like this intense and intoxicating journey leaves me almost breathless.

Now, my feet move faster. My heart beats louder. My arms stretch wider. My eyes see more vividly. And even my smile radiates brighter. I'm going to run until I wear out the soles on my shoes, and I am going to shine and leave a little light in every dark place I encounter. I have God on my side, so I cannot go wrong. Though I will continue to make mistakes and face challenges that I may not always overcome, I am still glad to be dancing to the rhythm of love while singing through the blues of life. You can't touch me!

God has activated my internal green light,

and now I talk, smell, taste, feel,

and see from within my soul.

SPIRITUAL REALM

I am so grateful to know that God has a purpose for my life. Knowing that God is merciful and that he still blesses me, I am humbled. In retrospect, a great source of my confusion was based upon the fact that every change in my life came during sporadic failures and losses. It was during these times that I barely met my personal needs and professional demands. Now, I understand that I was a bigger disappointment to myself than I ever was to God and my loved ones combined.

This epiphany in my life resulted from many contributing factors. My belief in divinity and knowing that God governs over my life was a major reason. Also, God revealed an internal, dormant truth in me that showed me how worthy I am to be alive to make mistakes, to learn from them, and to keep challenging myself to improve. In addition, God has given me the right of redemption to do something purposeful with the remainder of my life because I still have a strong mind, able body, and generous heart.

God revealed an internal, dormant truth in me

that showed me how worthy I am to be alive,

to make mistakes, to learn from them,

and to keep challenging myself to improve

**THE LOVE
ZONE**

"Run On"

My song **"Run On"** was paired up with the seventh elemental source in my body, potassium, at 0.35 percent. This element regulates the natural rhythm of my beating heart and transmits impulses through my central nervous system. Potassium also works with sulfur to keep my blood pressure stable.

My songs **"Forced Abstinence"** and **"Run On"** accomplish this very point; they both help me to focus and relax without high levels of stress and demands on my mind and body. They are both paramount to the realization of my commitment to live a positive, purposeful, and productive life.

STAGE THREE

Intuition

I. DICTIONARY

Intuition (noun)

Instinctive knowledge:
The state of being aware of or knowing something without having to discover or perceive it, or the ability to do this;

Instinctive belief:
Something known or believed instinctively, without actual evidence for it

Immediate knowledge:
PHILOSOPHY; immediate knowledge of something

    Related words/terms
- Intuitional (adjective)

II. THESAURUS

Instinct (noun)
- ★ Instinct
- ★ Perception
- ★ Insight
- ★ Sixth Sense

Hunch (noun)
- ★ Hunch
- ★ Feeling
- ★ Inkling
- ★ Suspicion
- ★ Sense
- ★ Presentiment

HOPE SPARKLES AGAIN

This song was my realization that though I needed love, I was still not ready to receive it.

Whenever you are near, I'm more inspired to persevere to claim a piece of the American dream and share with you everything.

When I was young, I dreamed that I would be a star; now, I dream to shine forever in your heart.

I'm revealing this because I can't believe you've come along so unexpectedly.

I'm still too skeptical to trust; yet, I find myself daydreaming about us.

I'm still denying myself someone to hold; I don't need the games, lies, or pain anymore.

Though I try to run you away, you address my needs and draw me near despite the things I say.

I'm cornered now by your love; I'm forced to deal with me; and this "to be or not to be" is so overwhelming.

Music and lyrics © Tiffany Samuel   *Performed by Tiffany Samuel*

56

7

Discovery Channel: Hope Sparkles Again
Season: Adversity

MENTAL REALM

Once full of self-pity,

which often felt more real

and potent than my desire to love,

I found myself overcome

with the reoccurrence of fear

that reappeared like a common cold,

and as a result, I chose to relent

and reject every opportunity to engage in love.

Channeling positive self-talk over and over again in my head, I recited these lines to wage a war against my lingering self-doubt as I stood looking into my bathroom mirror. "I'm a good person. I help people and not expect compensation. I forgive people and not judge them. I have a lot to offer an honorable, God-fearing man. I'm multitalented, well educated, physically fit, humorous, attractive, and I love God." Then, I lowered my head, not to pray, but in shame. I was doing it again. I was compensating for the absence of a mate by substituting qualities and attributes that I felt effectively excused, justified, waived, or vindicated my current status—single.

Whenever I felt judged by others or myself, I always became defensive. It seemed as though everyone I conversed with always had the same intrusive inquiries: "Girl, what are you waiting on? Aren't you getting a little too old to still be waiting on Mr. Right? Do you want to or plan to have children one day? Is something wrong with you? What's taking you so long?"

Once full of self-pity, which often felt more real and potent than my desire to love, I found myself overcome with the recurrence of fear that reappeared like a common cold, and as a result, I chose to relent and reject every opportunity to engage in love. Instead of participating in the game of life, I panicked, again. With any man's pitch of interest in a relationship with me, I just watched it fly by my home plate without even one swing of hope.

To this end, I had even convinced myself that if love was truly meant to come into my life, then it should not have a problem maneuvering through the strategically designed maze, trap, quicksand, and barbed wire erected around my fragile heart. Because I was not truly ready to commit on any level—mind, body, or spirit—unfortunately, I sabotaged most opportunities to make a real connection with someone who could possibly have enriched my life.

In retrospect, I did nothing except stall and waste time. *Valuable* time was lost! I became lethargic and unfocused. Failing to make the cognitive connection in my mind that my stubbornness only produced flawed reasoning and actions, I now realize that I subconsciously activated my "default button of destruction," which simultaneously deactivated my positive attitude, self-confidence, and self-efficacy, simply because I did nothing. Yes, I wrote this agonizing truth, and in case you missed my confession above: "What did I do to harm myself? I DID NOTHING TO CHANGE MY OUTCOME!"

PHYSICAL REALM

Convinced that both avoiding pain and coping with pain could still produce the same results, I erroneously relied on this rationale to validate my commitment to avoiding my problems. I stopped coping with my pain because I felt like I deserved a little hiatus from all the hard work. Just like a break on the job meant that I did not answer phones, complete tasks, or provide consultations, I took a "Cope No More/Love Hangover" break of equal measure. I gave up without a good reason. *Tired* was not a good reason.

Intending to just take a few days off from my self-improvement project, I allowed the days to turn into weeks and into months and finally into years. With all this elapsed time, I convinced myself that I was probably more healed and renewed than not, so I became complacent. Needless to say, my past issues reemerged with a vengeance and overwhelmed me, while I foolishly fell asleep at the wheel of hope.

I stopped coping with my pain

because I felt like I deserved a little hiatus

from all the hard work.

So why did I do all this work on my mind, body, and spirit if layers and layers and layers of my core kept revealing more and more and more issues and challenges still yet to be resolved? When would this roller-coaster ride filled with clandestine melancholy and sporadic paranoia finally end? When was I ever going to break through this cycle—and be happy? I was beyond feeling tired and disgusted with myself as this soap opera played over and over again in my subconscious mind.

SPIRITUAL REALM

In deep turmoil, the struggle to accept the notion that people, not love, can be flawed, sinful beings, and can thus bring the possibility of pleasure or pain, not to mention the possibility of inspiration or despair, was frightening. Though often consumed with the mere desire to be loved, I was still far more afraid that the experience might somehow prove too awkward to feel natural and normal, which is relative and should be defined by each individual. Nonetheless, I was confident that I lacked the requisite optimism and composure to identify someone else's genuine love for me. Therefore, I felt myself regressing again, because I just might strike out in the game of love.

I was so unaware and in denial of the real truth about myself. Profoundly scarred and bruised beyond my mind, body, and spirit, I had a gaping hole in my soul. Moreover, I was too ashamed and guarded to let anyone pierce the veil of my vulnerable state to try to love me. Tragically, I was struggling within myself—you guessed it, again!

Today, more practical and less dramatic,

I now believe that love is for those who are willing

to take a degree of risks to obtain a degree of rewards.

To adopt a new practice and philosophy about love, my struggle to change was excruciating. My standard belief about love had been that it was a less than advantageous risk with my proven record of losses; thus the higher probability of failure than success ratio was the perfect excuse to avoid the experience. Today, more practical and less dramatic, I now believe that love is for those who are willing to take a degree of risks to obtain a degree of rewards.

Moreover, my only challenge now was how to keep myself motivated throughout my endearing journey to one day meet my soul mate. The need for love was so overwhelming that I was constantly second-guessing myself and hindering my own progress. More research and self-study was needed.

I had to regroup and dust off my home plate and try again to play the game of life with focus. To forgive myself again and again was awkward. Struggling to catch up for lost time, how was anyone else expected to accept and love me when I felt too complicated for even myself?

Then the day finally arrived when I wanted love enough to change my approach. As hope began to emerge, I recognized my attitude and behavior had become more cordial, and I began to view men who expressed kindness and interest in me in a refreshing and intriguing way: as courageous and complex human beings, filled with hope and optimism for better things to come into their lives, just like me.

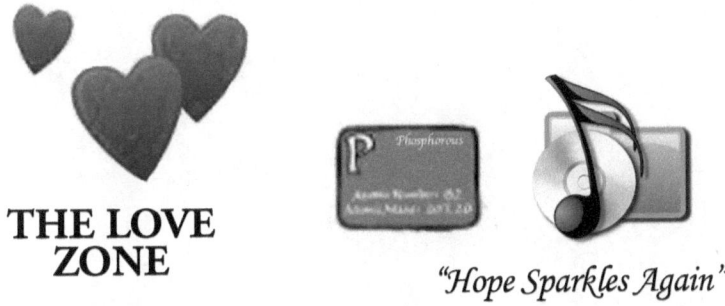

THE LOVE ZONE

"Hope Sparkles Again"

My song "**Hope Sparkles Again**" was paired up with the sixth elemental source in the human body, phosphorus. My body needs only 1 percent to boost the metabolic functions relating to my brain, muscle action, and nerves. Although God has taught me that with faith the size of a mustard seed, I can move mountains, I must still activate my faith in God through personal choice. Hope also requires the same initiative. And with hope, only a small amount is needed to spark a revolution in the soul.

AN AUTUMN NIGHT'S DREAM

This song was a beautiful dream that I believe can come true. By sharing this dream with the world, I have given it life:

Hear my love sigh;
See me on a love high;
Touch me until my body cries;
Taste me until I explode inside;
As the warmth flows from our ecstasy, smell the
*   sweet aromatherapy*
This on-time love can't be denied;
I gave up on love, and you brought it back to
*   my life.*

Music and lyrics © Tiffany Samuel   *Performed by Tiffany Samuel*

Discovery Channel: An Autumn Night's Dream
Season: Resilience

8

MENTAL REALM

This song was based upon a dream whereby I envisioned myself, futuristically, in the arms of my soul mate. Though I rarely dream, I was delighted by this wonderful surprise. During this dream, I felt suspended in time with an authentic, remarkable, inexplicable, and exhilarating mate who made me feel alive. Now, all I have to do is bring this dream to life, which reality stole from me as I began to open my eyes and stare into the darkness of my room. My imagination had taken me to a magical place and just left me there to sob in my loneliness for an hour. I felt cold and abandoned, and self-pleasure could not and was not an option for this profound emptiness.

During this dream,

I felt suspended in time with an authentic,

remarkable, inexplicable,

and exhilarating mate who made me feel alive.

To be clear, I do enjoy moments of self-pleasure; however, partner intimacy can still be equally if not more fulfilling. For this reason, I desire participation and energy from a mate, along with his love and humanity. I am not too old, too empowered, or too anything to want and need a man's love to enhance my own. As a result, most of my family and friends have labeled me a hopeless romantic.

Nonetheless, a community that encourages fellowship and love is what I believe in because people still need one another. Even with the high rate of broken families in our country, I believe we still want togetherness as human beings. In my opinion, humankind can still thrive because we were created out of God's love, and God desires to see his love grow and multiply.

Obedient to God's will, I pray to be able to know and accept the mate he chooses for me. Mainly because I will not subject myself to the possibility of a man's cavalier dismissal of our relationship and intimacy as a financial convenience, stress reliever or to simply satisfy his sexual appetite. This will not be my legacy to find love.

Consequently, when hope wins, I win. Now, on my journey with God, I accept this solo journey until I am led to a divine partnership. Moreover, I am grateful to have a self-love and acceptance that has given me more energy and courage to live authentically than I ever received from a partner in a relationship.

Why is this so? How is this possible? First, I know that I am loved because I have learned to invest in the daily practice of positive self-talk and self-love. Likewise, I know I am loveable because God has cultivated in me a high level of self-worth and self-respect. Moreover, I know that I am lovely because when I look at myself in the mirror, I smile so big and bold at myself that I have to wink and blow myself a big kiss.

PHYSICAL REALM

Still, what does this have to do with my potential soul mate? Simplistically, I am in love with who I am now; thus I do not want the wrong partner to come into my life and into my heart that could be counterproductive to my blossoming work in progress. Moreover, I love God, and undoubtedly, God loves me. Thus, I desire to be blessed with a loving mate to be chosen by God according to his standards. With great humility, I concede that I do not know how to choose a mate for myself. Thus, I would rather God chose my mate because he knows what is in a man's heart and what is right for me.

Please allow me to share an excerpt from my ventilation archives on my breakdown and breakthrough prayer sessions with God about my cares and concerns with a mate.

"I do not want a narcissistic, bitter, desperate, lazy, self-righteous, whore-monging, jealous, negative, pitiful or devilish man neither as a soul mate, nor business partner, nor friend, nor companion, nor spiritual confidante, etc."

"But that which I desire to have is a man who knows how to share all of his love and intimacy—from his soul with decency and respect for God and me."

I would rather God chose my mate,

because he knows what is in a man's heart

and what is right for me.

What some people settle for or accept as a mate: simply a warm body to hold on to at night or an extra paycheck to pay bills is unacceptable for me. This type of rationale can lead to engaging in a tumultuous, regret-filled relationship settlement agreement.

By my definition, a relationship settlement agreement sends the counterproductive message that each partner willingly chooses to digress from what they need and deserve and, in turn, both incur some degree of unnecessary risks and losses. Moreover, there is no specific performance requirement of love, respect and fidelity. Rather, there is only a pitiful exception clause added to revoke the agreement if either partner fails to maintain politeness and avoidance of all other issues without discussion. This settlement agreement is a lose-lose situation, because love is not a negotiation of exact services. Love requires infinite flexibility and fellowship to provide healthy solutions to daily challenges in life.

To the contrary, what I nicknamed as a relationship fusion agreement sends the constructive message that both partners understand and accept the sacrifices and rewards that come with mutual accountability and a strong work ethic. Likewise, both partners also seek to develop mutual respect and fortitude to love unconditionally and live with purpose and passion in their goal-driven friendship and partnership. This merger is a win-win situation, because fairness is paramount along with the commitment to love.

Still, during many discussions with various people on relationships, I have listened to people acknowledge that they settled for a marital arrangement or a cohabitation agreement because they began to age, needed financial assistance, struggled as a single parent, desired perpetual in-house sex in a committed relationship, or were just depressed and lonely in a house that did not feel like a home. Tragically, these flawed, loveless relationships only deprive the human spirit of growth and vitality. Every human being deserves to experience God's unconditional gift that lives within us all --- the ability to love one another.

SPIRITUAL REALM

After much contemplation and discussion, I adamantly renounce the group that I have fictitiously nicknamed the limited settlers group, and fully endorse the fictitious global fusion network because the notion that love has abandoned planet Earth and settled on the planet Venus is simply not true. Even if the thrill may be gone for most, love still awaits those who are patient and courageous enough to seize golden opportunities that are often present, but overlooked.

With all the love hangovers that spur from coast to coast, the once fun and exhilarating limbo dance of passion has now had its lowering bar of challenge completely removed from the social dating scene. As a result, there is no anticipation or reward. Instead, it appears that the new dance has become dart ball where the objective is to hit and claim any person that moves or bursts onto the scene as your mate and pitiful prize.

An extraordinary, unconditional love

from one human being to another

is not beyond God's power.

Nonetheless, I fervently believe that it is never too late to give and receive love. An extraordinary, unconditional love from one human being to another is not beyond God's power. Since God does not limit my ability to love and be loved, I can have and do hereby claim that an extraordinary, unconditional mate will come into my life. For this reason, I now close my ventilation archives on my paroxysm sessions with God. To this end, I will continue to reject subscriptions and memberships to the love is doomed network because I am a true believer in love.

With God's guidance, I realize that neither perfection

nor the answers to my questions are necessary

to follow God's divine instructions and obtain the rewards.

It does not matter that my past relationships were unhealthy nor does it matter that I still do not have all the answers to my questions about men. With God's guidance, I realize that neither perfection nor the answers to my questions are necessary to follow divine instructions and obtain the rewards. I just need to listen and learn as God guides me safely to my destination. My resilience keeps getting stronger because I choose to live, to love, and to believe time and time again.

THE LOVE ZONE

"An Autumn Night's Dream"

My song **"An Autumn Night's Dream"** is paired up with the fifth elemental source, calcium, which is in my body at 1.5 percent. This element accounts for two to three pounds of my total body mass. Also, calcium helps to build strong teeth and bones and regulates muscle growth.

On another note, calcium that is paired with my song **"An Autumn Night's Dream"** and magnesium that is paired with my song **"Don't Worry"** both work together to regulate the impulses in my central nervous system and the activation of various hormones and enzymes. This powerful duo also supports functions such as blood clotting and maintains blood pressure.

Consequently, I am more willing to move forward into a relationship filled with all the ingredients that will promote peace and support unity between my partner and me. This process has taught me that everything that makes me human also makes me humble. To maintain stability and encourage a spirit of forgiveness and cooperation in my future relationship, I have to support that union with all the pleasures I have been blessed and equipped with to cultivate an extraordinary life with my soul mate.

NUANCES

This song is about healthy choices. Whether we choose to improve or lose, life will still go on, and those that choose to rebuild can still find love.

She who hurts and heals is a strong woman.
He who forgets and forgives is a strong man.
If she lives and learns, she is a wise woman.
If he still cares and understands, he is a wise man.
She who prays by his side is a strong woman.
He who controls his manly pride is a strong man.
If she's positive after strife, she is a wise woman.
If he journeys from doing wrong to doing right, he is a wise man.

Music and lyrics © Tiffany Samuel   *Performed by Tiffany Samuel*

9

Discovery Channel: Nuances
Season: Metamorphosis

MENTAL REALM

I have often pondered this question: "If I had been given the power to foresee my future, would I have prevented some of my mistakes and failures?" Triumphantly, I can now proclaim, "I think not!" I understand now that without the trials of life, I would have no testimonies of success. Though I have cried through many painful past experiences, I can now laugh and have hope for my future. Major failures in my past have evolved into extraordinary testaments to my strength and desire to overcome adversity.

As a young girl, full of energy and curiosity, I observed my parents struggle with poverty, parenthood, debt, unbelievable odds on their jobs and entrepreneurship ventures, as well as cope with their own unfilled goals and plans, insecurities, and regrets. Still, I was blessed to have parents that were profoundly committed to one another and their children's future.

My parents were strategists, though I don't believe they knew it at the time, because they instilled in us a belief that our future was not limited by our low socioeconomic status in society. We had talent, and we valued our education. As a result, we believed that we could defy the cycle of poverty and, at times, felt invincible in school and in our community. We were achievers because my parents would not accept mediocrity. During the best of times, my parents were simply brilliant, wonderfully amazing, and our heroes. During the worst of times, my parents were inexplicably perplexed and in turmoil. Through it all, our family was both tragically unified and triumphantly human.

As a result, my parents gave us what they could—tough love, support, and a dream for a better life in hopes that we would acquire the additional resources and golden opportunities for infinite levels of success in college. Now, as a matured woman, I am full of wisdom and consciousness. To this end, I pray the Serenity Prayer daily for my parents and try to provide them with whatever they need for their wellness and support. For my beloved family, I pray for peace, healing, and closure over the things we cannot change.

I understand now that without the trials of life,

I would have no testimonies of success.

PHYSICAL REALM

Now evolving into a well-rounded person, my journey has molded me into the person I am today. Nonetheless, even though I enjoy a degree of success now, my initial journey was plagued with youthful trauma that I have sense learned to forgive and move beyond to heal. For example, as long as I adhered to perfect obedience in my parent's home, I was somewhat safe from their harsh discipline. Nonetheless, my curiosity would prove almost fatal in a home with strict parents like mine. I rarely talked to boys on the telephone. With school, church, chores, band practice, and the family business, there was little time to have fun with other kids.

Every challenge was always met with resistance,

because I could not predict the severity of the outcome.

Punishments always meant severe beatings with tree limbs, two-by-fours, broomsticks, fists, feet, and anything in the area to cause pain, followed by extra chores. The list of painful offenses included a grade of B or C on any school assignment and course based upon my parent's assessment of my effort; a boy anywhere in my vicinity; rebuttal comments, also known as talking back or disrespecting authority; unfinished chores; dancing; wearing makeup; experimenting and/or playing with any potentially harmful person, place, or thing based upon my parent's assessment of the circumstances; and any other infraction my parents deemed worthy of physical torture. Without a word to best describe my state of mind during that time, I will just concede that I was a miserable teenage girl—DEPRESSED!

Destined for college because my parents' motto was College or Death, I was glad to attend college because I was free from tyrannical rule. However, coping with my fears was never a part of my agenda. As a result, every challenge was always met with resistance because I could not predict the severity of the outcome. Moreover, I was done with punishment, pain, and consequences; thus, I was in defense mode and deathly afraid of everything and everyone.

College and apartment life also proved challenging. Anxiety became my companion when I struggled to balance my academic course load, scholarship, extracurricular obligations, multiple jobs, and a growing list of past due bills. Regretfully, I sometimes wrote checks for food or personal items though I knew there was not enough money in my bank account. Even worse, I resorted to lying to bill collectors about my identity or simply not answering calls from unidentified callers. Bill collectors left messages at all my jobs and past due bills were frequently sent to my apartment.

I was done with punishment, pain and consequences;

thus, I was in defense mode and deathly afraid

of everything and everyone---

because I could not predict the severity of the outcome.

SPIRITUAL REALM

The list could go on. However, today I can look back and feel a sense of accomplishment in my life mainly because if I could live with and through my shameful, painful past without bitterness and still have hope, I can certainly overcome any new challenges.

As I reminisce over my fears and tears, I realize that I ran so blindly from pain that I was oblivious to the falling bricks of low self-worth that stifled my constructive energy. Stumbling over and over again on my issues of self-doubt, I am overwhelmed today by how far I have traveled, how much I have learned, and how blessed I have been to survive it all and thrive despite it all. Only God's divinity over my life could produce this level of remarkable change and growth.

The once impossible notion of a second chance for success in my life is now my proclaimed destiny. A life filled with many beloved things is now my definition of success. Joy and happiness, understanding and forgiveness, peace and love, and encouragement and support are valuable attributes to living a healthy and purposeful life.

Only God's divinity over my life

could produce this level

of remarkable change and growth.

THE LOVE ZONE

"Nuances"

My song "**Nuances**" is paired up with the fourth elemental source, nitrogen, which is in my body at 3 percent. When my body generates nitrite through normal nitrogen metabolism, nitric oxide is produced. At normal levels, this element is a life-supporting biological messenger that helps heal wounds and burns, promotes blood clotting, controls blood pressure, enhances brain function, and boosts immunity to kill tumor cells and intracellular parasites. Also, nitrogen protects my stomach against food-borne pathogens.

Nuances, such as strength and wisdom, are important to my future because they provide me with positive internal powers to defeat negative external forces. With an obligation and responsibility to store up these qualities on a daily basis, I prepare to properly battle obstacles and challenges along my journey.

STAGE FOUR

Intimacy

I. DICTIONARY

Intimacy (noun)

Close relationship:
A close personal relationship;

Quiet atmosphere:
A quiet and private atmosphere;

Detailed knowledge:
A detailed knowledge resulting from a close and long association or study

Private utterance or action:
A private and personal utterance or action;

Sexual act:
A sexual act or sexual intercourse

- ♠ Often used euphemistically

II. THESAURUS

Familiarity (noun)
★Familiarity   ★Closeness   ★Understanding   ★Relationship
★Confidence

WISDOM

This song is my humble prayer request for a new beginning.

For a time, I seemed destined to fail.
Foolishly, I never planned or practiced to prevail.
I always traveled with small minds on hopeless roads to nowhere.
Now, I live my impossible dream with peace, love, and happiness.
I thought I needed someone to have and to hold;
So despair consumed my heart without the courage to let go.
I stayed too long and caused myself needless heartache and misery.
Now, I refuse to waste more time, and I've changed my priorities.

Music and lyrics© Tiffany Samuel   *Performed by Tiffany Samuel*

10

Discovery Channel: Wisdom
Season: Adversity

MENTAL REALM

This channel was the catalyst that sparked my eventual breakthrough from an endless cycle of unfulfilled love. Though I still wandered off in my silent pain at the sight of mothers playing with their children and couples displaying affection as I observed them at the movies, at the grocery store, or at various community events, I was determined not to let my inner pain culminate into an impromptu public meltdown for an unsuspecting audience. To add insult to injury, I had experienced this overwhelming longing to bond and relentless aching for affection during my first channel, *promises*, yet now, it resurfaced for a somewhat different reason.

Intrusive and disturbingly antagonistic,

I could not enjoy my usual quiet time alone

for meditation and renewal.

Ready to bond and feel needed by someone, this felt different from just wanting love. Wanting to bond and to have a routine and mutual obligation to nurture and support in a team environment, this felt like loneliness. Intrusive and disturbingly antagonistic, I could not enjoy my usual quiet time alone for meditation and renewal. Several years ago, I used to rely on promises from others to give me a pseudo sense of love. Baffled by this startling irony, I began to pout and whimper similar to that of a restless infant, desiring to be perpetually cradled by a nurturing mother. Nervous as uncontrollable feelings began to surface sporadically, like mini tantrums, I was certain everyone could see the internal conflict raging within my heart and mind in search of someone to love.

During this awkward time, I experimented with yet another approach to love. My strategy was to use reverse psychology to get what I wanted. I decided to love everyone without requiring reciprocation because most people always seemed to do the opposite of what I expected them to do anyway. This was my brilliant attempt to receive love by pretending like I did not need love in return. This nonchalant approach was, in theory, projected to reward me tenfold with more love than my heart or hands could hold. Today, I still don't know why this ridiculous analogy was considered plausible. Needless again to say, the outcome was confusion and rejection.

Love was treated like a scientific experiment, a mathematical equation, a charitable cause, or a musical or artistic masterpiece of great complexity. My rationale during this period in my life was very closely compared to the lyrics of a song by music legend Teddy Pendergrass entitled "Love TKO." The lyrics describe how Teddy's approach to love was so foolish, because he continued to produce the same negative results—pain, rejection, and loss. Understanding this issue now, I realize that I was in denial by believing that I was not making the same mistakes that Teddy had sung about. Silly me, I was Teddy's virtual backup singer, and I did not even realize it.

Even worse, I tried to apply logic to my failed relationships because I believed that they required an analytical approach. This was yet another past issue that required a resolution. With every new day, I guard myself against falling into these same troublesome approaches to love and happiness.

PHYSICAL REALM

Now that I have matured and have begun the healing process, I ask myself this question: "Self, what have you learned thus far in your life about love?" One such lesson on love is to appreciate love from sources other than human beings, such as the special relationship I shared with my two dogs, Dominique and Patra. I am a true dog lover.

Dominique and Patra never told my secrets,

lied, cheated, or stole things from me

like people had done to me.

To begin, my two dogs proved to be more authentic and unconditional than any relationship I have ever had with a person. My dogs provided stability for me for two-thirds of my adult life. For example, they witnessed most of my growing pains through college, job promotions, relationships, finances, personal injuries, solitude, and friendships. Also, Dominique and Patra were so forgiving, predictable, and welcoming whenever I came home. Even when I could not always physically or financially provide them with the best care and nutrition, my dogs seemed to love me more.

Dominique and Patra were my best friends, and we were a team. All I had to do was give them my best effort, and they responded to me with love. They gave me so much attention and love that I found myself satisfied with our utopia for a few years. Most days, I hurried to complete my work so I could return home to play with my dogs. I even missed classes during college to take long walks and picnics with Dominique and Patra. I performed mini concerts for them and even trained them to howl the happy birthday song for family and friends. I wanted to spend my daytime hours with people so at night my dogs and I could curl up in bed and watch movies until we fell asleep. I enjoyed this uninterrupted, peaceful time in my life. Dominique and Patra never told my secrets, lied, cheated, or stole things from me like people had done to me.

When I lost Patra to breast cancer, she was nearly ten years old in human years. With the devastation of her loss, her veterinarian assigned me a grief counselor to comfort me. Patra was young and had no prior health problems. I just knew we would have so many years together to build memories. After her death, I was pretty miserable. With the holiday season approaching, I did not feel like celebrating.

Then, the next devastation came. I lost Dominique to kidney failure two months later. He was almost fifteen years old in human years. Then, it happened. I had a good old-fashioned nervous breakdown.

A few years before Dominique's death, he had suffered from hip dysplasia, and thus he walked around in a mobility cart. I had the cart made especially for him, and it allowed Dominique to walk with little to no assistance. Also, he had been taking arthritis medication for about two years after he endured a stroke, home therapy, and a long rehabilitation period. Dominique was a fighter, yet he seemed depressed without Patra. He was constantly digging through the carpet, looking under beds, behind doors, into closets and out of the windows for something or someone. When his veterinarian told me to keep a close eye on him after Patra's death for signs of depression, I was sure that problem already existed.

I tried everything to keep him from looking around the house for Patra. My mother even came to stay with Dominique for a week while I continued to work, but Dominique's spirits remained somber. Consequently, I had little to no peace, and after his death, I had to move out of the place that no longer felt like a home. With acceptance of their deaths, I can still love them and smile when I see their puppies. More than companions and protectors, my dogs were nurturers and a pure gift from nature to generate my love and respect for life.

Another lesson learned about love is to celebrate and not mourn when a life is given back to God. Now, I have the strength to celebrate the lives of my deceased family and friends because I now honor how they taught me, encouraged me, protected me, labored with me, and loved me with joy and gratitude. The memories of all the love we shared are certainly worth celebrating and not regretting with sorrow and misery. Now I understand why it is important to embrace fond memories during and after a loved one's death. I choose not to be selfish and angry when I know that a loved one has received eternal peace and an end to their suffering.

Nothing will last forever, and no one will live forever. Life requires a transfer of energy from one state into another—life until death. I believe that my loved ones have given me more desire to love and live to fulfill their legacies.

SPIRITUAL REALM

Though I had spent many years in search of another person's love and affection, little did I know that sometimes God's work can be a source of inexplicable mystery and awesome power. Since learning that love does not always reveal itself in the source I desire, I began to recognize how God was healing me through manifestations of love in other forms of his creation. With new understanding and appreciation for the tangible things around me every day, I am grateful.

The birth of my intimacy

was the result of a very simple phenomenon:

I began to return the love that was given to me

from the sources that gave it freely.

This revelation and acceptance of a special yet neglected gift from God made me think about all the times I prayed in error and accusation to God by asking, "When am I going to receive love, God? How can I keep praying to you and not receive an answer, God? Why won't you just give me another chance to love, God?" Now, I pray a different prayer: "Please forgive me, God, for I know not what I was saying or doing." God had shown me great love, yet I was not aligned with him to understand and receive it. Like a kid with a new toy, I began to whisper about God's love offering to me as if it was a well-guarded secret: reciprocity from nature!

The birth of my intimacy was the result of a very simple phenomenon: I began to return the love that was given to me from the sources that gave it freely. The irony was that the love I desired was there all the time through nature. When I nurtured my plants, they grew. Whenever I fed my dogs, they ate and then curled up beside me thereafter and slept. When I played music or sang, the chords and sounds calmed my spirit. Likewise, water therapy and recreational activities seemed to transform me from whatever mood, thought, or feeling I had into a tranquil state of relaxation.

From these experiences, I was awakened to a better understanding of what motivates and inspires me to want to be a better person who copes with her problems instead of denies them. With more focus on what brought me more appreciation and love, I began to redefine what wisdom meant to me. Wisdom was no longer simply the mastery of avoiding the same mistakes and acquiring the expertise to effectively deal with people and life situations. Wisdom now meant how to invest in myself as a priority because I am worth it. Also, it meant that I had a responsibility to understand my strengths and weakness and safeguard and caution myself when making decisions and live with purpose and passion to help others.

THE LOVE ZONE

"Wisdom"

My song **"Wisdom"** is paired up with the third elemental source, hydrogen, which is in my body at 10 percent. The basis of water, hydrogen, is the universal solvent and medium of chemistry. Hydrogen allows my body to effectively absorb water just like wisdom allows my brain to make better decisions. Therefore, they are both critical to my ability to succeed.

Wisdom has calmed my life and given me more confidence. Hydrogen has replenished my body and given me all the water I need for proper bodily functions and digestion. I am grateful for these self-improvements and life lessons.

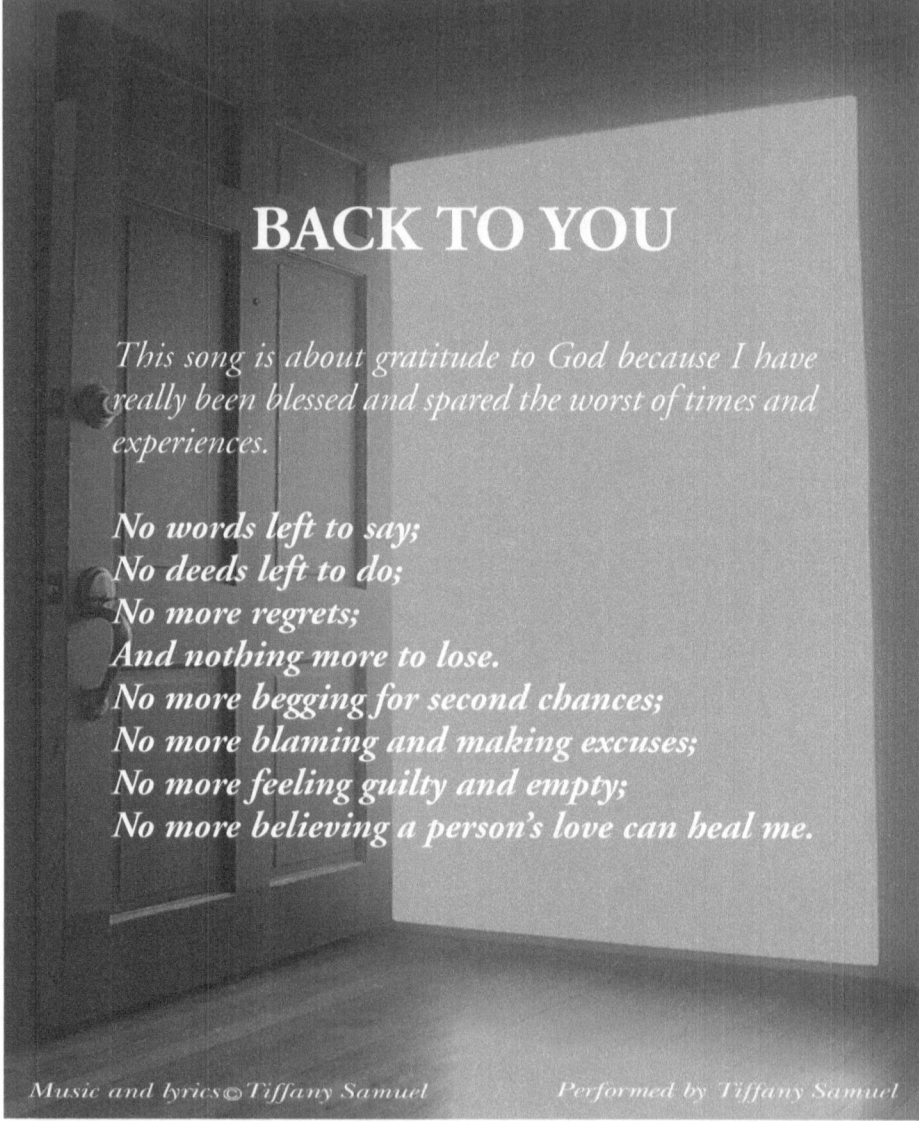

BACK TO YOU

This song is about gratitude to God because I have really been blessed and spared the worst of times and experiences.

No words left to say;
No deeds left to do;
No more regrets;
And nothing more to lose.
No more begging for second chances;
No more blaming and making excuses;
No more feeling guilty and empty;
No more believing a person's love can heal me.

Music and lyrics © Tiffany Samuel   *Performed by Tiffany Samuel*

11

Discovery Channel: Back To You
Season: Resilience

MENTAL REALM

A little bit of every channel shares my journey to reconnect with God. I was wrong about many things, many people, and what I thought was valuable. Though I believed in God, I was not a true believer in God's ultimate powers to affect my life. Why would I write this in my journal? Primarily because, the whole truth about my relationship with God is that I was ill prepared and unwilling to serve God during disappointment.

Today, God has lovingly given me another chance when most people would not be so forgiving. Every day, I witness God's grace and experience daily his faithfulness. God understands and heals me beyond the ability of any human being. God has restored my courage and hope in a refreshing and unique way. These are not just words because I know that I could have been dead or spiritually lost and wandering the streets like so many people who still search for something real to believe in and to give them hope.

I was wrong about many things,

many people

and what I thought was valuable.

Now, the greatest motivation for my heart and mind to live free and with purpose is God. Reflecting again on my childhood, I acknowledge that I gave my heart to God, yet not my mind. Naïve about the challenges and obstacles ahead of me on my journey, I wanted to make my own decisions. As a result, I endured mental overload and anguish that affected my behavior and decisions. Since my heart was in God's hands, I believed I was safe, yet I was very wrong.

My conscious could not always prevent me from making bad decisions because my thoughts were not aligned with those of God. For the same reason, my words were not always positive or motivating. Focused on small matters that never encouraged my growth and success, I lived without adequate quality and substance to help me set goals and priorities for better living.

PHYSICAL REALM

Tired of waiting on God, I chose to believe only in what was tangible because I felt that God allowed people and the world I was living in to destroy me. Regretfully, I just believed that God chose to let bad things happen to me. This was my lowest period because I blamed God for everything.

I really feared everything and everyone

because the outcome seemed to always end the same:

pain, pain and more pain.

As a result, my lifestyle, conversation, and thoughts became more self-destructive. I was less God-fearing and more pain-fearing. I really feared everything and everyone because the outcome seemed to always end the same: pain, pain, and more pain. Therefore, God was not that extraordinary or well respected by default. Regretfully, I feared pain more than I loved and feared God. In turmoil with God, I began to disbelieve that God could save me.

SPIRITUAL REALM

No longer obligated to explain or justify my decisions regarding my life or my journey to find love, God is my only judge. Now, I have a more authentic relationship with God, and I celebrate our relationship in different ways. Sometimes, I sing a song of tribute, read a scripture, write an inspirational poem or love letter, share my testimony, forgive myself, forgive others, pray for wisdom and guidance, and try to live for God because he is forever present with me. Therefore, I have an even closer relationship now because I acknowledge his closeness. He is my personal savior.

On this journey, I am compelled to keep moving. I now travel with God as a free soul, an infinite traveler, an excited explorer, and a motivated journey woman. I accept my salvation and understand that I have a duty to share God's love with others. I love and serve God just like the birds that fly above, openly and freely. I am in love with God because he has convinced my mind and convicted my heart.

If I had given myself completely to God, I would have been spiritually free a long time ago. Brokenhearted, I foolishly gave too much of myself to people instead. With others in control of me, I was depressed and spiritually dead.

If I had given myself completely to God,

I would have been spiritually free a long time ago.

THE LOVE ZONE

"Back To You"

My song "**Back to You**" is paired up with the second elemental source, carbon, which is in my body at 18 percent. Carbon reacts either as a positive or negative atom, and it assumes whichever role is needed. Moreover, carbon is the skeletal framework for my bones and body chemistry. Accordingly, it lies in the middle of all things, and it attracts oxygen, which is the basis of life. Finally, carbon is self-organizing, whether the scale is small or large.

God is the creator of all things, and carbon is his elemental source and creation to restore life to everything. I do not need a research scientist, mathematician, academic scholar, or medical expert to tell me that God is real. A miracle happens on the planet every day because of the great works of God.

I know that no man can do what God can do. Moreover, I know that no creation will ever be greater than its creator. God gave me carbon to remind me to always stay close to his powerful source of healing and restoration. ***Back to You*** has finally brought me back where I belong, with God.

SOARING

This song was a self-affirmation to keep believing and moving toward a divine success in my life.

Lessons of life have taught me, and I take the joy and pain completely.
Now is my "little engine that could" ready for a place in history.
My travels have not been all good to me; still I have survived and made the best of things.
I've changed my list of things I need.
Control is real, and I live drama free.
I don't need anyone to give me what God gives unconditionally.
The difference that I see is a whole Tiffany emerging.

Music and lyrics © Tiffany Samuel   *Performed by Tiffany Samuel*

Discovery Channel: Soaring Season: Metamorphosis

12

MENTAL REALM

All this joy that I describe did not occur overnight. My joy took all my adult life to achieve in addition to everything I can channel from within daily to continue to overcome myself and stay aligned with God. Though people have tried to break my spirit, I realize that I gave people access and opportunity to cause me harm. I allowed my own demise because I was so willingly caught up, burnt out, heartbroken, sorry, and lost that I self-destructed.

I ran from light because I was

full of pain and low self-worth.

No longer desiring to control my destiny, I try my best to stay aligned with God. It sometimes seems scary to envision my own success because I have been self-destructive for years. Have you ever been in the dark so long that you cannot stand for someone to turn on a light? I ran from light because I was full of pain and low self-worth.

God uses everybody for something important. Important tasks may not always produce material wealth because sometimes God needs average means to produce powerful ends. I was an average believer, but now I am a powerful example of God's ability to save and restore a lost soul.

PHYSICAL REALM

The song that coincides with this channel is a pure melody and message of love in my heart. This channel is not about fixing me or even proclaiming my new beginning. This song is about accepting a profound love after refusing, denying, abusing, and neglecting my relationship with God and myself.

Head over heels in love with myself today,

I know that I am special and treasured by God.

So many times, I have disappointed God. Yet God loves and forgives me. Head over heels in love with myself today, I know that I am special and treasured by God. I have never felt special or received special treatment by a human being to the level of God's adoration of me. I am God's work in progress; God's beautiful soul; and God's masterpiece of change. Blessed to move beyond my pain, my present experiences are filled with hope. My future is auspicious.

I am God's work in progress;

God's beautiful soul;

and God's masterpiece of change.

Without a partner in life, I am tremendously blessed to be surrounded with a community of love from family and friends. While continuing to work on more self-improvements in my life, I can affirm that for every life issue God has an answer. As I have become more faithful to God, he has renewed my energy.

SPIRITUAL REALM

Twelve songs were chosen for my music disc from a diverse genre of songs that I have written from well over a decade. These songs were inspired by God to send a message of peace, forgiveness, goodwill, and love. Likewise, I believe that my twelve discovery channels were also inspired by God in a divinely perfect way. My music disc **Changing Tempos™** is God's answer to restoring unto me everything I have been denied.

Songs chosen were reflective of God's perfect and pure love for me; thus, there are no songs of vindication or to cause shame or harm to anyone. Rather, I sing and share my journey of redemption from victimization to love. To illustrate love as I saw it then and as I see it now, I share my life chords, soul rhythms, and heartfelt lyrics.

With an amazing grace,

I know that only God can save

and deliver a person who is spiritually lost.

When people tell me that spirituality is unfounded and illogical, I can relate to them because I was once spiritually low as well. Yet through God's mercy, I was spared the worst, which is to battle with self-destruction and lose my soul and belief in him. With an amazing grace, I know that only God can save and deliver a person who is spiritually lost. I am God's living example of a spiritual resurrection of hope.

God *is* my personal savior. Meeting God on the brink of my demise, I know and embrace God in all his greatness. I have come out of the darkness of doubt and disbelief to know and love God authentically. I love myself better because God has taught me how to love him better. My prayer is that every day another soul will break free from every person, place, or thing that binds or hinders their ability to soar in love with God and unlock their destinies.

I love myself better

because God has taught me how to love him better.

THE LOVE ZONE

"Soaring"

My song "**Soaring**" is paired up with the first elemental source, oxygen, which is in my body at 65 percent. Oxygen is the activator of hydrogen in water. Also, oxygen is the balance in oxidation and reduction reactions. Needless to say, without oxygen, we could not breathe, and thus, we could not live. I love the purity of oxygen. No matter what I have learned and shared about my life in this journal book, nothing would have been accomplished without this final channel.

God took me through an oxidation process. Full of substances that guaranteed my continuous failure, I needed God's purification of my spirit. God also took me through a reduction process. Misled by untimely and uncoordinated reactions to love, life, and loss, I needed God's reconstruction of my mind, body, and spirit to learn forgiveness, fortitude, and faith. Another obstacle that needed God's correction was my unwillingness to reconnect and renew my personal relationship with the Trinity over my life: God (the Father), Jesus Christ (his Son), and the Holy Spirit. If there was ever a time that I needed a source so powerful and life changing, the time is now.

This beautiful mind and emerging spirit that God has given me requires less worry and more forgiveness of others and of myself. My new beginning is now full of privilege and purpose. Privileged to have a second chance to live a better life with health and wellness as a foundation; to be alive and still value the simple things in life, such as laughter, nature, and friendship; and to accept that pain is a natural, unavoidable consequence of living and learning how to survive without giving into fear. Now, I am full of a more realistic purpose. I am here to do my best to represent the principles and values of my creator, and I am here to share and receive love. It is not my job to fix, correct, redirect, and punish those who chose to use the vessel of love to harm or hinder me on my journey, whether out of their ignorance or intent. Instead, I succeed every time I respond with more courage and love. I have finally arrived, and love is my destiny. This love *is* forever! Peace.

Love Zone: "Reader Ponders"

Directions: Now it is your turn to journal. Answer the love questions on the lines provided below.

♥ WHO IS LOVE?

Author: This is simple for me. In my opinion, **GOD is love**. So since God is in me, I should have the ultimate gift to share. Yet this unconditional gift was counter-offered in my past, unhealthy relationships with a purchase agreement and addendum of special conditions that must be met before it could be fulfilled.

Reader*:*

_____

_____

_____

_____

_____

_____

_____

♥♥ WHAT IS LOVE?

Author: If it is a **feeling**, then I must be clogged due to poor circulation. If it is a **taste**, then maybe I have a taste bud condition like ageusia. If it is a **sound**, then maybe the hearing aid test was in error, and I really am deaf. If it is a **sight**, then I had better stay in at night because I must be "blind as a bat." And if it is a **smell**, then add a condition like anosmia to my cart because when I inhale, there is nothing there.

Reader:

_____

_____

_____

_____

_____

_____

_____

♥♥♥ *WHEN IS IT THE RIGHT TIME TO LOVE?*

Author: Now! My cold hands and feet need a cuddling mate. Confused birds sit down beside me and just stare because they do not know what to sing to me, "Close to You" or "Green Sleeves." **Now, I say . . . Now is the time!**
Reader:

_____

_____

_____

_____

_____

_____

_____

♥♥♥♥ *WHERE IS LOVE?*

Author: Apparently, **love is everywhere**. However, I can only substantiate pure love **from nature**. For example, I love water and thus indulge in swimming, playing in the rain, bathing for hours, and listening to its sound. Nonetheless, my first love of nature is music, and it is still my ultimate expression of love.
Reader:

_____

_____

_____

_____

_____

_____

♥♥♥♥♥ *WHY DO WE NEED LOVE?*

Author: Well, I seek love because I want to bond with others for an additional source of energy and purpose. Also, I know that I **do not want to be alone forever!** Nonetheless, I also know that I need my personal space at times to replenish my mind, body, and soul in my own way. So . . . I wait.
Reader:

_____

_____

_____

_____

_____

_____

_____

♥♥♥♥♥♥ *HOW DO WE LOVE?*

Author: I am not sure. Is love **math and science?** Is love **arts and humanities?** In my opinion, love is universally infinite. Thus, I desire another authentic and open soul to journey with me to embrace love! Until then, I'll be here . . . waiting!
Reader:

_____

_____

_____

_____

_____

_____

_____